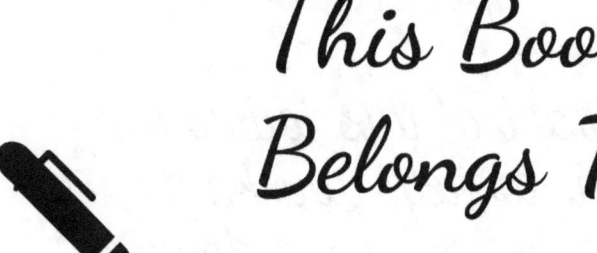

This Book Belongs To:

"There is nothing to writing. All you do is sit down at a typewriter and bleed." Ernest Hemingway

This Journal is made of two parts;

First part of this journal is meant to help you know yourself better, write down in great detail as much as you can by answering the questions.

Second part is designed for daily use, fill your morning pages with love everyday.

Set A Writing Goal Today.

Make writing a part of your identity.

 ────────────────

WRITING PROMPT

WHAT YOU DID YESTERDAY?

YOUR PLANS FOR TODAY

© Copyright 2021 - All rights reserved.
You may not reproduce, duplicate or send the contents of this book without direct written permission from the author. You cannot hereby despite any circumstance blame the publisher or hold him or her to legal responsibility for any reparation, compensations, or monetary forfeiture owing to the information included herein, either in a direct or an indirect way.

Legal Notice: This book has copyright protection. You can use the book for personal purpose. You should not sell, use, alter, distribute, quote, take excerpts or paraphrase in part or whole the material contained in this book without obtaining the permission of the author first.

Disclaimer Notice: You must take note that the information in this document is for casual reading and entertainment purposes only. We have made every attempt to provide accurate, up to date and reliable information. We do not express or imply guarantees of any kind. The persons who read admit that the writer is not occupied in giving legal, financial, medical or other advice. We put this book content by sourcing various places.

Please consult a licensed professional before you try any techniques shown in this book. By going through this document, the book lover comes to an agreement that under no situation is the author accountable for any forfeiture, direct or indirect, which they may incur because of the use of material contained in this document, including, but not limited to, —errors, omissions, or inaccuracies.

WRITING PROMPT

AN INSPIRING BOOK, FILM OR ALBUM YOU HAVE ENCOUNTER

WRITING PROMPT

LESSONS YOU'VE LEARNED FROM A COURSE YOU TOOK

WRITING PROMPT

HOW YOU'RE FEELING TODAY

WRITING PROMPT

AN ARGUMENT YOU HAD AND WHAT WERE THE CHALLENGES YOU FACED

WRITING PROMPT

A MEMORY FROM YOUR PAST

WRITING PROMPT

WHAT ARE YOUR DREAMS

WRITING PROMPT

HOW DO YOU PROGRESS TOWARDS A GOAL

WRITING PROMPT

A PROBLEM IN YOUR LIFE THAT DISTRACTS YOU FROM YOUR DREAMS AND PROGRESS

WRITING PROMPT

YOU ARE GIVEN THE CHANCE TO TRAVEL BACK TO ANY POINT IN YOUR LIFE TO DO THINGS DIFFERENTLY.
WHAT POINT DO YOU CHOOSE?
WHAT DO YOU DO DIFFERENTLY AND HOW DOES IT AFFECT YOU NOW?

WRITING PROMPT

WHAT IS THE HAPPIEST MEMORY YOU HAVE FROM CHILDHOOD? DESCRIBE IT IN GREAT DETAIL.

_____
_____
_____
_____
_____
_____
_____
_____
_____
_____

WRITING PROMPT

WHAT DOES THE CONCEPT OF HOME MEAN TO YOU? WRITE IN GREAT DETAIL WHERE YOU MOST FEEL AT HOME.

WRITING PROMPT

WHAT IS SUCCESS FOR YOU? TALK ABOUT WHEN YOU FELT MOST ACCOMPLISHED, PROFESSIONALLY AND PERSONALLY.

WRITING PROMPT

TALK ABOUT A TIME WHEN YOU FELT LIKE A FAILURE AND HOW DID THIS EXPERIENCE HELPED YOU PROGRESS.

SECOND PART OF THIS JOURNAL IS FOR YOUR DAILY USE, KEEP YOUR DAILY MORNING PAGES WITH A LIGHT HEART AND AN OPEN-MIND.

DAY

DAY

DAY

DAY

DAY

DAY

DAY

DAY

DAY

DAY

DAY

DAY

DAY

DAY

DAY

DAY

DAY

DAY

DAY

DAY

DAY

DAY

DAY

DAY

DAY

DAY

DAY

DAY

DAY

DAY

DAY

DAY

DAY

DAY

"GREAT CREATIVE MINDS THINK LIKE ARTISTS BUT WORK LIKE ACCOUNTANTS."
DAVID BROOKS

www.ingramcontent.com/pod-product-compliance
Lightning Source LLC
LaVergne TN
LVHW020135080526
838202LV00047B/3941